The Sampler Blanket

30 Knit Squares - 30 Stitch Patterns

Lisa Hoffman

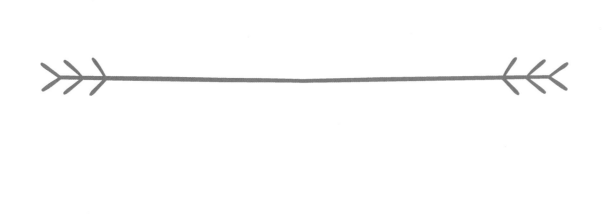

The Sampler Blanket by Lisa Hoffman

Introduction

For many years, this 30 pattern sampler blanket has been a favorite project with my students. The pattern has been revised and updated with charts and photographs added for each square along with the written pattern descriptions.

From Advanced Beginner to the more Experienced knitter this is a skill building project introducing new techniques as it is worked. It is a fun and exciting project, enriching the knitter with a great sense of accomplishment as each square is completed and a new one begins. The blanket is knit in 5 strips, each with 6 patterns. The strips are then crocheted together, and finished with a crochet trim.

In addition, there is a schematic for a 12 square Baby Blanket that uses fun textured patterns with a stockinette square for monogramming.

Table of Contents

Materials

Approximately 2000 yards of worsted weight yarn.
US 7 (4.5mm) needles, or size needed for your gauge.
Crochet Hook 4.5/G, or size needed for your gauge.
Stitch markers/Cable needle/Darning needle.
 *For a Baby or Stroller blanket using the same 30 squares, use approximately 1500
yards of a DK weight yarn and comparable needle/hook size. For a 12 square blanket Baby or Stroller
blanket using worsted weight yarn, plan on approximately 1000 yards. See page 23.

Gauge

(Gauge is important only to determine the finished size of your blanket)
18 sts x 26 rows = 4″ in Stockinette Stitch for sample shown.

Finished Measurements

45″ x 54″ for full size afghan sample shown [each pattern approx. 9″ square] knit in String Classica
(50g/1.75oz) 125y/115m 100% Cashmere, 16 skeins, color 419 Light Teal.

24″ x 32″ for baby blanket sample shown [each pattern approx. 8″ square] on page 28 knit in Koigu Emmi
(50g/1.75oz) 130y/118m , 75% Merino/25% Cashmere, 7 skeins, color E906.

Pattern Notes
Please read before beginning your project

The blanket has 30 different patterns, worked in 5 separate strips with 6 patterns each. For each strip, the
pattern squares are each bound off, then stitches are picked up for the following square. The strips are
crocheted together, and the blanket is finished with a crochet border.

Each of the patterns in the 5 strips is worked with a garter selvedge. This is one extra knit stitch beyond
the pattern on the RS and WS at each end of every row. These 2 extra stitches are included in the stitch
counts, but NOT in the individual patterns. This way you can choose to use these same stitch patterns
for other projects.

Some patterns are reversible. To remember which is the RS (right side) vs the WS (wrong side), place
a removable marker or scrap yarn on the RS of your work.

See page 4 for a full schematic of the 30 pattern layout.

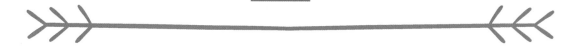

Abbreviations

BO Bind off.

C4b (Cable 4 back) Slip next 2 sts onto cable needle, hold to back, knit 2 sts from left hand needle, then knit the 2 sts from the cable needle.

C4f (Cable 4 front) Slip next 2 sts onto cable needle, hold to front, knit 2 sts from left hand needle, then knit the 2 sts from the cable needle.

Cdd (Center double decrease) Slip 2 sts together knitwise, k1, pass 2 slipped sts over.

K2tog Knit 2 sts together.

K3tog Knit 3 sts together.

M3 Make 3 sts by knitting into the front, back and front of stitch.

P3tog Purl 3 sts together.

Sc Single crochet.

Sl1 Slip 1 stitch knitwise, unless otherwise specified in pattern.

S1k2p Slip1 stitch knitwise, knit 2 sts (not together), pass 1 slipped stitch over 2 knit sts.

Sl1wyib Slip1 stitch purlwise with yarn in back.

Sl1wyif Slip1 stitch purlwise with yarn in front.

Ssk Slip1 stitch knitwise, slip next stitch as if to knit, knit those 2 sts together through back loops.

Sts Stitches.

T4b (Twist 4 back) Slip next 2 sts onto cable needle and hold in back, knit 2 sts from left hand needle, then purl the 2 sts from cable needle.

T4f (Twist 4 front) Slip next 2 sts onto cable needle and hold in front, purl 2 sts from left hand needle, then knit the 2 sts from cable needle.

Yo Yarn over.

Sampler Blanket Chart Key

K Knit **P Purl** RS Knit. RS Purl. WS Purl. WS Knit.	**No Stitch**	**O** **YO - Yarn Over** Bring yarn around the needle to make 1 st.	**W** **M3 - Make 3** Increase 2 sts by knitting into the front/back/front.
K2tog Knit 2 sts together.	**Ssk - Slip slip knit** Slip1 st knitwise, slip next knitwise, knit the slipped sts tog through back loops.	**Sl1 wyif** Slip1 st purlwise with yarn in front.	**Sl1 wyib** Slip1 st purlwise with yarn in back.
K3tog Knit 3 sts together.	**³⁄.** **P3tog** Purl 3 sts together.	**K2tog tbl** Knit 2 sts together through the back loops.	**Cdd - Center** **Double Decrease** Slip 2 sts together knitwise, k1, pass 2 slipped sts over.
C4f - Cable 4 front Slip 2 sts to cable needle, hold to front, k2, k2 from cable needle.	**C4b - Cable 4 back** Slip 2 sts to cable needle, hold to back, k2, k2 from cable needle.	**T4f - Twist 4 front** Slip 2 sts to cable needle, hold to front, p2, k2 from cable needle.	**T4b - Twist 4 back** Slip 2 sts to cable needle, hold to back, k2, p2 from cable needle.
S1k2p Slip 1 st knitwise, knit each of the next 2 sts individually (not together) then pass the slipped st over the 2 knit sts.	**Popcorn** See instructions on Pattern 13.	**M** **M1 Make 1** Make 1 st by lifting up the bar before next st to the left needle and knitting into it to make a hole - not a twisted st.	**Knot** See instructions on Pattern 28.

Sampler Blanket Schematic

Fir Cone **Pattern 30**	Harris Tweed **Pattern 24**	Little Arrowhead **Pattern 18**	Lattice **Pattern 12**	Pebble **Pattern 6**
Wavy Rib **Pattern 29**	Staggered Eyelets **Pattern 23**	Purl Triangles **Pattern 17**	Slip Stitch Waffle Rib **Pattern 11**	Knotted Cables **Pattern 5**
Knots **Pattern 28**	Cheques **Pattern 22**	Mock Eyelet Cable Rib **Pattern 16**	Slanted Seed Rib **Pattern 10**	Bramble **Pattern 4**
Double Fleck **Pattern 27**	Layette Lace **Pattern 21**	Mirrored Twists **Pattern 15**	Diagonal Lace **Pattern 9**	Slanted Rib **Pattern 3**
Alternate Lace **Pattern 26**	Diamond Brocade **Pattern 20**	Eyelet Ridges **Pattern 14**	Alternate Parallelograms **Pattern 8**	Little Shell **Pattern 2**
King Charles Brocade **Pattern 25**	Cable & Lace **Pattern 19**	Popcorn **Pattern 13**	Double Lace Rib **Pattern 7**	Seed Dots **Pattern 1**

Instructions

Please read this entire section before beginning.

Starting with Pattern 1, cast on 41 sts. Knit 1, place marker, work first row of pattern 1, place marker, knit 1. Continue pattern 1 for 48 total rows, slipping markers and knitting 1st and last selvedge stitches. Remove markers on the bind off row.

Bind off loosely with RS (right side) facing (note that all squares are bound off on RS) leaving last stitch on the needle. Turn. With WS (wrong side) facing, pick up under both strands of each of the stitches just bound off (the first stitch, left on needle, counts as 1 stitch).

You will always have one stitch less than the stitch count from the previous pattern. This is because the first 2 sts complete a single bind off. Stitches for the next pattern are always picked up with WS facing. Always count your sts after you pick up. A ridge appears on the RS of the blanket, mimicking the look of a crochet edge, separating patterns.

If the next pattern has more or less stitches than the previous pattern you need to increase or decrease evenly spaced along the first row of the new pattern. If pattern directions do not indicate how to increase or decrease on the first row, increase by Kf/b (knitting into the front and back of a stitch), decrease by K2tog (knitting 2 together).

Replace selvedge markers at Row 1 of each new pattern.

Continue as established until the strip is six patterns long. Bind off loosely.

Change yarn at the end of a skein or ball at the beginning or end of a row so yarn tails can be woven into the crocheted seams in finishing. A tip to keep the selvedge edges neat and easy to crochet is to end 2 sts into a row or before the end of a row. **Do not darn ends until all pieces are complete.** See Finishing for more details.

Work the four remaining strips.

You can work the patterns in the order they are presented or switch them around if you like. You might want to work one strategically placed square in Stockinette stitch to personalize with initials by overstitching or embroidery in the finishing.

ADDITIONAL NOTE The patterns are written to reflect the repeats on the charts. A row that reads R1 *K4, p1, k3; rep from * means to k7 between the p1 sts until the end of the repeat, ending with k3.

For every pattern every row remember to work the selvedge sts as follows:
Knit one, slip first marker, work pattern to last marker, slip marker, knit one.

Pattern 1 · Seed Dots

(multiples of 10 + 9 sts)
39 sts + 2 selvedge = 41 sts.

Row 1 ∗K4, p1, k5; rep from ∗ to last 9 sts, k4, p1, k4.
Row 2 Purl.
Row 3 ∗K9, p1; rep from ∗ to last 9 sts, k9.
Row 4 Purl.
Repeat these 4 rows 12 times (48 rows). Bind off knitwise.

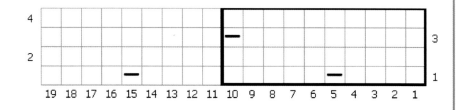

Pattern 2 · Little Shell

(multiples of 7 + 2)
37 stitches + 2 selvedge = 39 stitches

Row 1 Knit
Row 2 Purl
Row 3 K2, ∗yo, p1, p3tog, p1, yo, k2; rep from∗ to end
Row 4 Purl
Repeat these 4 rows 12 times (48 rows). Bind off knitwise.

 P3tog Purl 3 sts together.

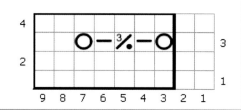

For every pattern every row remember to work the selvedge sts as follows:
Knit one, slip first marker, work pattern to last marker, slip marker, knit one.

Pattern 3 · Slanted Rib

(multiples of 4 + 2 sts)
38 sts + 2 selvedge = 40 sts.

Row 1 K2, *p2, k2; rep from * to end.
Row 2 and all wrong side rows Work stitches as
they appear.
Row 3 K1, *p2, k2; rep from * to last st, p1.
Row 5 *P2, k2; rep from * to last 2 sts, p2.
Row 7 P1, *k2, p2; repeat from * to last st, k1.
Row 8 As row 2.
Repeat these 8 rows 6 times (48 rows). Bind off in pattern as Row 1.

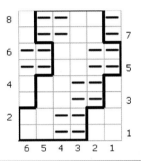

Pattern 4 · Bramble

(multiples of 2 sts)
42 sts + 2 selvedge = 44 sts.

Rows 1 and 3 Purl.
Row 2 P1, *m3, p3tog; repeat from * to last stitch, p1.
Row 4 P1, *p3tog, m3; repeat from * to last stitch, p1.
Repeat these 4 rows 11 times (44 rows). Bind off purlwise.

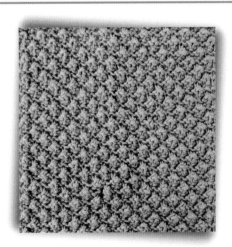

 P3tog Purl 3 sts together.

 M3 Make 3
Increase 2 sts by knitting into the front/back/front.

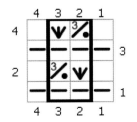

For every pattern every row remember to work the selvedge sts as follows:
Knit one, slip first marker, work pattern to last marker, slip marker, knit one.

Pattern 5 · Knotted Cables

(multiples of 10 + 3 sts)
43 sts + 2 selvedge = 45 sts.

Rows 1,3,7 *P2, k4, p2, k2; repeat from * to last 3 sts, p3.
Row 2 and all WS rows Work stitches as they appear.
Row 5 *P2, C4b, p2, k2; repeat from * to last 3 sts, p3.
Rows 9 P1, *p2, k2, p2, k4; repeat from * to last 2 sts, p2.
Row 11 P1, *p2, k2, p2, k4; repeat from * to last 2 sts, p2.
Row 13 P1, *p2, k2, p2, C4f; repeat from * to last 2 sts, p2.
Row 15 P1, *p2, k2, p2, k4; repeat from * to last 2 sts, p2.
Row 16 *K2, p4, k2, p2; repeat from * to last 3 sts, k3.
Repeat these 16 rows 3 times (48 rows). Bind off in pattern as Row 15.

 C4b Cable 4 back
Slip 2 sts onto cable needle, hold to back, knit 2 sts from left
hand needle then knit the 2 sts from the cable needle.

C4f Cable 4 front
Slip 2 sts onto cable needle, hold to front, knit 2 sts from left
hand needle then knit the 2 sts from the cable needle.

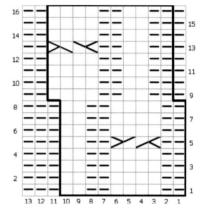

Pattern 6 · Pebble

(multiples of 2 sts)
36 sts + 2 selvedge = 38 sts.

Rows 1 Knit.
Rows 2 Purl.
Rows 3 *K2tog; repeat from * to end.
Row 4 *K1, pick up horizontal bar before next stitch
and knit it; repeat from * to end.
Row 5 Knit
Row 6 Purl
Row 7 *K2tog; repeat from * to end.
Row 8 *M1, k1; repeat from * to end.
Repeat these 8 rows 7 times, then rows 1-4 once (60 rows).
Bind off knitwise.

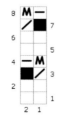

M M1 Make 1 st by lifting the horizontal bar before next stitch and knit into it.

For every pattern every row remember to work the selvedge sts as follows:
Knit one, slip first marker, work pattern to last marker, slip marker, knit one.

Pattern 7 · Double Lace Rib

Rib (multiples of 6 + 2 sts)
38 sts + 2 selvedge = 40 sts.

Row 1 K2, *p1, yo, k2tog tbl, p1, k2;
repeat from * to end.
Row 2 P2 *k1, p2, k1, p2; repeat from * to end.
Row 3 K2, *p1, k2tog, yo, p1, k2; repeat from * to end.
Row 4 P2 *k1, p2, k1, p2; repeat from * to end.
Repeat these 4 rows 12 times (48 rows). Bind off knitwise.

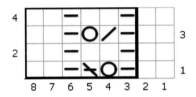

 K2tog tbl Knit 2 sts together through the back loops.

Pattern 8 · Alternate Parallelograms

(multiples of 10 sts)
40 sts + 2 selvedge = 42 sts.

Row 1 P5, *k5, p5; rep from * to last 5 sts, k5.
Row 2 K1, p5, *k5, p5; rep from * to last 4 sts, k4.
Row 3 P3, *k5, p5; rep from * to last 7 sts, k5, p2.
Row 4 K3, p5, *k5, p5; rep from * to last 2 sts, k2.
Row 5 P1, *k5, p5; rep from * to last 9 sts, k5, p4.
Row 6 P4, k5, *p5, k5; rep from * to last st, p1.
Row 7 K2, *p5, k5; rep from * to last 8 sts, p5, k3.
Row 8 P2, k5, *p5, k5; rep from * to last 3 sts, p3.
Row 9 K4, *p5, k5; rep from * to last 6 sts, p5, k1.
Row 10 K5, *p5, k5; rep from * to last 5 sts, p5.
Repeat these 10 rows 4 times, then rows 1-5 once.
Purl one row (46 rows). Bind off knitwise.

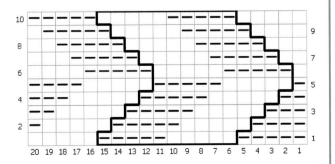

For every pattern every row remember to work the selvedge sts as follows:
Knit one, slip first marker, work pattern to last marker, slip marker, knit one.

Pattern 9 · Diagonal Lace

(multiples of 5 + 4 sts)
39 sts + 2 selvedge = 41 sts.

Row 1 K1, *k2tog, yo, k3; rep from * to last 3 sts, k2tog, yo, k1.
Row 2 P3, *k3, p2; rep from * to last st, p1.
Row 3 K5, *k2tog, yo, k3: rep from * to last 4 sts, k2tog, yo, k2.
Row 4 P1, k1, p2, *k3, p2; rep from * to end.
Row 5 K4, *k2tog, yo, k3; rep from * to end.
Row 6 P1, k2, p2, *k3, p2; rep from * to last 4 sts, k3, p1.
Row 7 K3, *k2tog, yo, k3; rep from * to last st, k1.
Row 8 P1, *k3, p2; rep from * to last 3 sts, k2, p1.
Row 9 K2, *k2tog, yo, k3; rep from * to last 2 sts, k2.
Row 10 P2, *k3, p2; rep from * to last 2 sts, k1, p1.
Repeat these 10 rows 5 times (50 rows). Bind off knitwise.

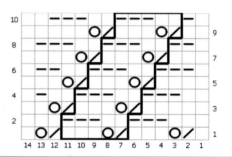

Pattern 10 · Slanted Seed Rib

(multiples of 6 sts)
36 sts + 2 selvedge = 38 sts.

Row 1 *K5, p1; rep from * to end.
Row 2 P1, *k1, p5, rep from * to last 5 sts, k1, p4.
Row 3 K3, p1, *k5, p1; rep from * to last 2 sts, k2.
Row 4 P3, *k1, p5; rep from * to last 3 sts, k1, p2.
Row 5 K1, p1, *k5, p1; rep from * to last 4 sts, k4.
Row 6 P5, *k1, p5; rep from * to last st, k1.
Repeat these 6 rows 8 times (48 rows). Bind off in pattern as Row 1.

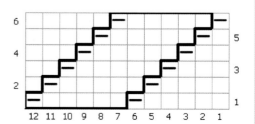

For every pattern every row remember to work the selvedge sts as follows:
Knit one, slip first marker, work pattern to last marker, slip marker, knit one.

Pattern 11 · Slip Stitch Waffle Rib

(multiples of 6 + 3 sts)
39 sts + 2 selvedge = 41 sts.

Note Slip st purlwise with yarn in back.

Row 1 *K3, Sl1wyib; repeat from * to last 3 sts, k3.
Row 2 K3, *p1, k3; rep from * to end.
Row 3 *P3, Sl1wyib; rep from * to last 3 sts, p3.
Row 4 K3, *p1, k3; rep from * to end.
Row 5 *P3, Sl1wyib; rep from * to last 3 sts, p3.
Row 6 K3, *p1, k3; rep from * to end.
Row 7 *P3, Sl1wyib; rep from * to last 3 sts, p3.
Row 8 K3, *p1, k3; rep from * to end.
Row 9 *K3, Sl1wyib; repeat from * to last 3 sts, k3.
Row 10 Purl.
Repeat these 10 rows 4 times, then rows 1-8 once (48 rows). Bind off knitwise.

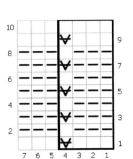

Sl 1 wyib Slip 1 st with yarn in back.

Pattern 12 · Lattice

(multiples of 12 + 2 sts)
50 sts + 2 selvedge = 52 sts.

Set up Row 1 Work first row as a knit row with increases as follows
from 40 sts - K1 (selv), [k2, kf/b] 12 times, k2, k1 (selv) - 52 sts.
Set up Row 2 Purl.

After the increase proceed to work rows 3 - 8.
On following repeats begin from Row 1 as written.

Row 1 K1, *C4b, p2; rep from * to last st, k1.
Row 2 and all WS rows Works sts as they appear.
Row 3 K1, p2, *k2, T4b; rep from * to last 5 sts, k5. .
Row 5 K1, *P2, C4f; rep from * to last st, k1.
Row 7 K3, *k2, T4f, rep from * to last 5 sts, k2, p2, k1.
Row 8 Work sts as they appear.
Repeat these 8 rows 6 times (48 rows).
Bind off *BO 2 sts, k2tog, BO; rep from * to end.

T4b Twist 4 back Slip 2 sts to cn and hold to back,
k2 from left needle then p2 from cn.

T4f Twist 4 front Slip 2 sts to cn and hold to front,
p2 from left needle then k2 from cn.

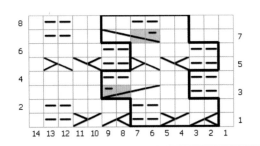

For every pattern every row remember to work the selvedge sts as follows:
Knit one, slip first marker, work pattern to last marker, slip marker, knit one.

Pattern 13 · Popcorn

(multiples of 6 + 5 sts)
35 sts + 2 selvedge = 37 sts.

Row 1 Knit.
Row 2 Purl.
Row 3 K2, *make Popcorn, k5; rep from * to last 3 sts, make Popcorn, k2.
Row 4 Purl.
Row 5 Knit.
Row 6 Purl.
Row 7 K5, *make Popcorn, k5; rep from * to last 6 sts, make Popcorn, k5.
Row 8 Purl.
Repeat these 8 rows 6 times (48 rows). Bind off knitwise.

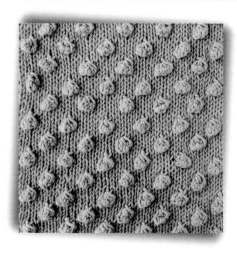

 Make Popcorn Knit in front and back of next st 2 times (4 sts), turn,
p4, turn, k4, then working one st at a time pass (as if to BO) 2nd, 3rd,
and 4th st over the 1st st. Push Popcorn to the RS of work, knit
the next st tightly.

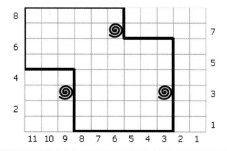

Pattern 14 · Eyelet Ridges

(multiples of 2 + 3 sts)
39 sts + 2 selvedge = 41 sts.

Note YO row is on Row 4 which is a WS row.

Row 1 Knit.
Row 2 Purl.
Row 3 Knit.
Row 4 K2, *yo, k2tog; rep from * to last st, k1.
Row 5 Knit.
Row 6 Purl.
Repeat these 6 rows 8 times (48 rows). Bind off knitwise.

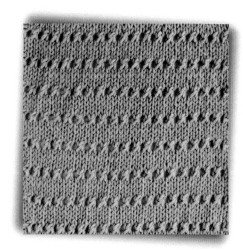

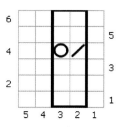

For every pattern every row remember to work the selvedge sts as follows:
Knit one, slip first marker, work pattern to last marker, slip marker, knit one.

Pattern 15 · Mirrored Twists

(multiples of 11 + 2 sts)
46 sts + 2 selvedge = 48 sts.

Note Because of the large # of sts to increase, work row 1 of the first repeat
as follows: P2, *, Inc, k2, p1, Inc, k2, p2; rep from * 3 times more.
(Inc by knitting into the front and back of the next stitch)

After the increase proceed to work row 2.
On following repeats work Row 1 as written.

Row 1 P2, *k4, p1, k4, p2; rep from * to end.
Row 2 K2, *p4, k1, p4, k2; rep from * to end.
Row 3 P2, *sl2 wyib, k2, p1, k2, sl2 wyib, p2; rep from * to end.
Row 4 K2, *sl2 wyif, p2, k1, p2, sl2 wyif, k2; rep from * to end.
Row 5 P2, *T4f, p1, T4b, p2; rep from * to end.
Row 6 K2, *p4, k1, p4, k2; rep from * to end.
Repeat these 6 rows 9 times (54 rows).
Bind off To reduce the large number of sts, decrease 8 sts by binding
off knitwise after Row 6 by k2tog in the middle of each twist cable. 39 sts.

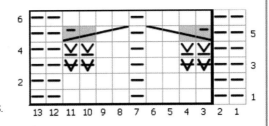

T4f Twist 4 front Slip 2 sts to cn and hold to front,
p2 from left needle then k2 from cn.

T4b Twist 4 back Slip 2 sts to cn and hold to back,
k2 from left needle then p2 from cn.

V Sl1 wyif
Slip 1 st purlwise with yarn in front

V Sl1 wyib
Slip 1 st purlwise with yarn in back

Pattern 16 · Mock Eyelet Cable Rib

(multiples of 5 + 4 sts)
39 sts + 2 selvedge = 41 sts.

Note The stitch count changes from Rows 1 to 2.

Row 1 P3, *s1k2p, p2; rep from * to last st, p1. (32 sts)
Row 2 K1, *k2, p1, yo, p1; rep from * to last 3 sts, k3. (39 sts)
Row 3 P3, *k3, p2; rep from * to last st, p1.
Row 4 K1, *k2, p3, rep from * to last 3 sts, k3.
Repeat these 4 rows 12 times (48 rows). Bind off knitwise.

 S1k2p Slip 1, knit 2, psso
Sl1 st purlwise with yarn in back, k each of next 2 sts individually
(not together), pass slipped st over the 2 knit sts. 1 st decreased.

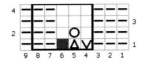

The Sampler Blanket by Lisa Hoffman

For every pattern every row remember to work the selvedge sts as follows:
Knit one, slip first marker, work pattern to last marker, slip marker, knit one.

Pattern 17 · Purl Triangles

(multiples of 16+ 5 sts)
37 sts + 2 selvedge = 39 sts.

Row 1 K3, *p7, k1; rep from * to last 10 sts, p7, k3.
Row 2 P3, k7, *p1; k7; rep from * to last 3 sts, p3.
Row 3 K4, *p5, k3; rep from * to last 9 sts, p5, k4.
Row 4 P4, k5, *p3; k5; rep from * to last 4 sts, p4.
Row 5 K5, *p3, k5; rep from * to end.
Row 6 *P5, k3; rep from * to last 5 sts, p5.
Row 7 K6, *p1, k7; rep from * to last 7 sts, p1, k6.
Row 8 P6, k1, *p7 k1; rep from * to last 6 sts, p6.
Row 9 P6, *k1, p7; rep from * to last 7 sts, k1, p6.
Row 10 K6, p1, *k7, p1; rep from * to last 6 sts, k6.
Row 11 P5, *k3, p5; rep from * to end.
Row 12 *K5, p3; rep from last 5 sts, k5.
Row 13 P4, * k5, p3; rep from * to last 9 sts, k5, p4.
Row 14 K4, p5, *k3, p5; rep from * to last 4 sts, k4.
Row 15 P3, *k7, p1; rep from * to last 10 sts, k7, p3.
Row 16 K3, p7, *k1, p7; rep from * to last 3 sts, k3.
Repeat these 16 rows 3 times (48 rows). Bind off knitwise.

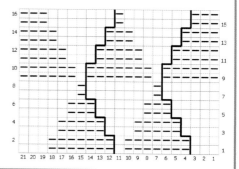

Pattern 18 · Little Arrowhead

(multiples of 6 + 3 sts)
33 sts + 2 selvedge = 35 sts.

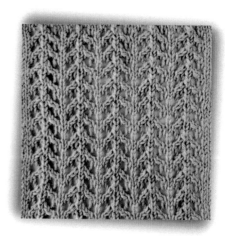

Row 1 K2, *yo, ssk, k1, k2tog, yo, k1; rep from * to last st, k1.
Row 2 Purl.
Row 3 K2, *k1, yo, cdd, yo, k2; rep from * to last st, k1.
Row 4 Purl.
Repeat these 4 rows 12 times (48 rows). Bind off knitwise.

 Cdd Center double decrease
Slip 2 sts together knitwise, k1, pass 2 slipped sts over.

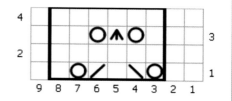

For every pattern every row remember to work the selvedge sts as follows:
Knit one, slip first marker, work pattern to last marker, slip marker, knit one.

Pattern 19 · Cable & Lace

(multiples of 10 + 4 sts)
44 sts + 2 selvedge = 46 sts.

Row 1 K1, k2tog, yo, *p2, k4, p2, k2tog, yo; rep from * to last st, k1.
Row 2 P1, *p2, k2, p4, k2; rep from * to last 3 sts, p3.
Row 3 K1, yo, ssk, *p2, C4f, p2, yo, ssk; rep from * to last st, k1.
Row 4 P1, *p2, k2, p4, k2; rep from * to last 3 sts, p3.
Row 5 K1, k2tog, yo, *p2, k4, p2, k2tog, yo; rep from * to last st, k1.
Row 6 P1, *p2, k2, p4, k2; rep from * to last 3 sts, p3.
Row 7 K1, yo, ssk, *p2, k4, p2, yo, ssk; rep from * to last st, k1.
Row 8 P1, *p2, k2, p4, k2; rep from * to last 3 sts, p3.
Row 9 K1, k2tog, yo, *p2, C4f, p2, k2tog, yo; rep from * to last st, k1.
Row 10 P1, *p2, k2, p4, k2; rep from * to last 3 sts, p3.
Row 11 K1, yo, ssk, *p2, k4, p2, yo, ssk; rep from * to last st, k1.
Row 12 P1, *p2, k2, p4, k2; rep from * to last 3 sts, p3.
Repeat these 12 rows 4 times (48 rows). Bind off knitwise.

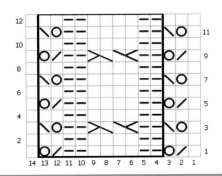

Pattern 20 · Diamond Brocade

(multiples of 8 + 1 sts)
41 sts + 2 selvedge = 43 sts.

Row 1 *K4, p1, k3; rep to last st, k1.
Row 2 P1 *p2, k1, p1, k1, p3; rep from * to end.
Row 3 *K2, p1, k3, p1, k1; rep from * to last st, k1.
Row 4 P1,*k1, p5, k1, p1; rep from * to end.
Row 5 *P1, k7; rep from * to last st, p1.
Row 6 P1,*k1, p5, k1, p1; rep from * to end.
Row 7 *K2, p1, k3, p1, k1; rep from * to last st, k1.
Row 8 P1, *p2, k1, p1, k1, p3; rep from * to end.
Repeat these 8 rows 6 times (48 rows). Bind off in pattern as Row 1.

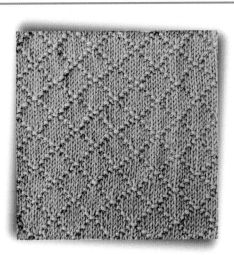

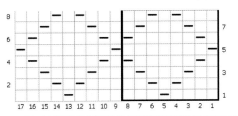

For every pattern every row remember to work the selvedge sts as follows:
Knit one, slip first marker, work pattern to last marker, slip marker, knit one.

Pattern 21 · Layette Lace

(multiples of 4 + 3 sts)

39 sts + 2 selvedge = 41 sts.

Row 1 P1, k1, p1, *p1, k3; rep from * to last 4 sts, p2, k1, p1.
Row 2 P1, k1, p1, k1, *p3, k1; rep from * to last 3sts, p1, k1, p1.
Row 3 P1, k2tog, yo, *p1, yo, k3tog, yo; rep from * to
last 4 sts, p1, yo, k2tog, p1.
Row 4 P1, k1, p2, *p1, k1, p2; rep from * to last 3 sts, p1, k1, p1.
Row 5 P1, k1, *k3, p1; rep from * to last 5 sts, k4, p1.
Row 6 P1, k1, p3, *k1, p3; rep from * to last 2 sts, k1, p1.
Row 7 P1, k1, *yo, k3tog, yo, p1; rep from * to
last 5 sts, yo, k3tog, yo, k1, p1.
Row 8 P1, *k1, p3; rep from * to last 2 sts, k1, p1,
Repeat these 8 rows 6 times (48 rows). Bind off knitwise.

 K3tog Knit 3 sts together

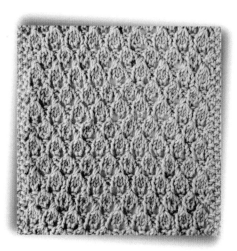

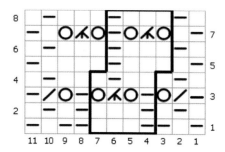

Pattern 22 · Cheques

(multiples of 8 + 2 sts)

38 sts + 2 selvedge = 40 sts.

Row 1 K5, p4, *k4, p4; rep from * to last 5 sts, k5.
Row 2 P5, k4, *p4, k4; rep from * to last 5 sts, p5.
Row 3 K5, p4, *k4, p4; rep from * to last 5 sts, k5.
Row 4 P5, k4, *p4, k4; rep from * to last 5 sts, p5.
Row 5 P5, k4, *p4, k4; rep from * to last 5 sts, p5.
Row 6 K5, p4, *k4, p4; rep from * to last 5 sts, k5.
Row 7 P5, k4, *p4, k4; rep from * to last 5 sts, p5.
Row 8 K5, p4, *k4, p4; rep from * to last 5 sts, k5.
Repeat these 8 rows 6 times (48 rows). Bind off knitwise.

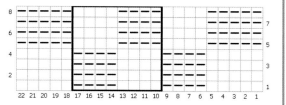

For every pattern every row remember to work the selvedge sts as follows:
Knit one, slip first marker, work pattern to last marker, slip marker, knit one.

Pattern 23 · Staggered Eyelets

(multiples of 6+ 3 sts)

33 sts + 2 selvedge = 35 sts.

Note Repeat is rows 3-6 only.

Setup Row 1 Knit
Setup Row 2 Purl
Row 3 K3, *k2tog, yo, k2; rep from * to last 2sts. k2.
Row 4 Purl.
Row 5 K1, *k2tog, yo, k2; rep from * to end.
Row 6 Purl.
Repeat Rows 3-6 12 times. (50 rows).
Bind off knitwise.

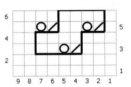

Pattern 24 · Harris Tweed

(multiples of 6 + 3 sts)

39 sts + 2 selvedge = 41 sts.

Row 1 Knit.
Row 2 Purl.
Row 3 *K3, p3; rep from * to last 3 sts, k3.
Row 4 P3, *k3, p3; rep from * to end.
Row 5 *K3, p3; rep from * to last 3 sts, k3.
Row 6 Knit.
Row 7 Purl.
Row 8 Knit.
Row 9 *K3, p3; rep from * to last 3 sts, k3.
Row 10 P3, *k3, p3; rep from * to end.
Row 11 *K3, p3; rep from * to last 3 sts, k3.
Row 12 Purl.
Repeat these 12 rows 4 times (48 rows). Bind off knitwise.

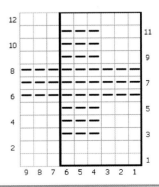

For every pattern every row remember to work the selvedge sts as follows:
Knit one, slip first marker, work pattern to last marker, slip marker, knit one.

Pattern 25 · King Charles Brocade

(multiples of 12 + 1 sts)
37 sts + 2 selvedge = 39 sts.

Row 1 *K1, p1, k9, p1; rep from * to last st, k1.
Row 2 K1, *p1, k1, p7, k1, p1, k1; rep from * to end.
Row 3 *[K1, p1] 2 times, k5, p1, k1, p1; rep from * to last st, k1.
Row 4 P1, *[p1, k1] 2 times, p2; rep from * to end.
Row 5 *K3, [p1, k1] 3 times, p1, k2; rep from * to last st, k1.
Row 6 P1, *p3, [k1, p1] 3 times, p3; rep from * to end.
Row 7 *K5, p1, k1, p1, k4; rep from * to last st, k1.
Row 8 P1 *p3, [k1, p1] 2 times, k1, p4; rep from * to end.
Row 9 *K3, [p1, k1] 3 times, p1, k2; rep from * to last st, k1.
Row 10 P1, *[p1, k1] 2 times, p2; rep from * to end.
Row 11 *[K1, p1] 2 times, k5, p1, k1, p1; rep from * to last st, k1.
Row 12 K1, *p1, k1, p7, k1, p1, k1; rep from * to end.
Repeat these 12 rows 4 times (48 rows). Bind off knitwise.

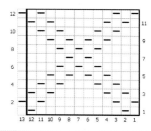

Pattern 26 · Alternating Lace

(multiples of 6 + 3 sts)
35 sts + 2 selvedge = 37sts.

Row 1 K1, *yo, cdd, yo, k3; rep from * to last 4 sts, yo, cdd, yo, k1.
Row 2 and all WS rows Purl
Row 3 K1, *yo, cdd, yo, k3; rep from * to last 4 sts, yo, cdd, yo, k1.
Row 5 K1, *yo, cdd, yo, k3; rep from * to last 4 sts, yo, cdd, yo, k1.
Row 7 K1, *yo, cdd, yo, k3; rep from * to last 4 sts, yo, cdd, yo, k1.
Row 9 K1, *k3, yo, cdd, yo; rep from * to last 4 sts, k4.
Row 11 K1, *k3, yo, cdd, yo; rep from * to last 4 sts, k4.
Row 13 K1, *k3, yo, cdd, yo; rep from * to last 4 sts, k4.
Row 15 K1, *k3, yo, cdd, yo; rep from * to last 4 sts, k4.
Row 16 Purl.
Repeat these 16 rows 3 times (48 rows). Bind off knitwise.

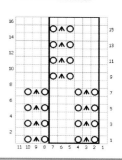

For every pattern every row remember to work the selvedge sts as follows:
Knit one, slip first marker, work pattern to last marker, slip marker, knit one.

Pattern 27 · Double Fleck

(multiples of 6 + 4 sts)
40 sts + 2 selvedge = 42 sts

Row 1 Knit
Row 2 P4, *k2, p4; rep from * to end.
Row 3 Knit
Row 4 P1, *k2, p4; rep from * to last 3 sts, k2, p1.
Repeat these 4 rows 12 times (48 rows). Bind off knitwise.

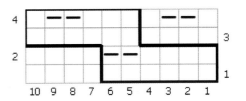

Pattern 28 · Knots

(multiples of 6 + 5 sts)
41 sts + 2 selvedge = 43 sts.

Row 1 Knit
Row 2 Purl
Row 3 K1, *knot, k3; rep from * to last 4 sts, knot, k1.
Row 4 Purl.
Row 5 Knit.
Row 6 Purl. .
Row 7 K4, * knot, k3; rep from * to last st, k1.
Row 8 Purl.
Repeat these 8 rows 6 times (48 rows). Bind off knitwise.

 Knot
P3tog leaving sts on left hand needle, bring yarn to back
and knit same 3 sts together, bring yarn to front and purl
same 3 sts together again, slip 3 sts off to right hand needle.

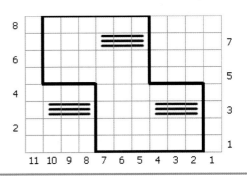

The Sampler Blanket by Lisa Hoffman

For every pattern every row remember to work the selvedge sts as follows:
Knit one, slip first marker, work pattern to last marker, slip marker, knit one.

Pattern 29 · Wavy Rib

(multiples of 6 + 4 sts)

40 sts + 2 selvedge = 42 sts

Row 1 P3, *k4, p2; rep from * to last 7 sts, k4, p3.
Row 2 K3, *p4, k2; rep from * to last 7 sts, p4, k3.
Row 3 P3, *k4, p2; rep from * to last 7 sts, k4, p3.
Row 4 K3, *p4, k2; rep from * to last 7 sts, p4, k3.
Row 5 *K4, p2; rep from * to last 4 sts, k4.
Row 6 *P4, k2,; rep from * to last 4 sts, p4.
Row 7 *K4, p2; rep from * to last 4 sts, k4.
Row 8 *P4, k2,; rep from * to last 4 sts, p4.
Repeat these 8 rows 6 times (48 rows). Bind off knitwise.

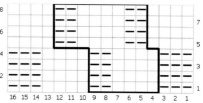

Pattern 30 · Fir Cone

(multiples of 10+ 9 sts)

39 sts + 2 selvedge = 41 sts.

Setup Work 4 rows of Stockinette st.
Row 1 K5, *yo, k3, cdd, k3, yo, k1; rep from * to last 4 sts, k4.
Row 2 and all WS Rows Purl.
Row 3 K5, *yo, k3, cdd, k3, yo, k1; rep from * to last 4 sts, k4.
Row 5 K5, *yo, k3, cdd, k3, yo, k1; rep from * to last 4 sts, k4.
Row 7 K5, *yo, k3, cdd, k3, yo, k1; rep from * to last 4 sts, k4.
Row 9 K4, k2tog, k3, yo, k1, *yo, k3, cdd, k3, yo, k1; rep from * to last 9 sts, yo, k3, ssk, k4.
Row 11 K4, k2tog, k3, yo, k1, *yo, k3, cdd, k3, yo, k1; rep from * to last 9 sts, yo, k3, ssk, k4.
Row 13 K4, k2tog, k3, yo, k1, *yo, k3, cdd, k3, yo, k1; rep from * to last 9 sts, yo, k3, ssk, k4..
Row 15 K4, k2tog, k3, yo, k1, *yo, k3, cdd, k3, yo, k1; rep from * to last 9 sts, yo, k3, ssk, k4.
Row 16 Purl.
Repeat these 16 rows 2 times, then row 1-8 once.
Finish Work 4 rows of Stockinette st (48 rows). Bind off knitwise.

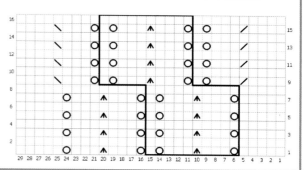

Finishing

Steam or wet block each strip. **Do not darn ends until after pieces are joined**. See bullet points below.

Match pieces according to the schematic on page 1. Strips are crocheted together from bottom to top. The method here will produce a centered (not slanted) crochet line.

Lay pieces with RS facing, with Strip 2 to the left of Strip 1. You will now be working into the space between the knots of the selvedge edge.

Using crochet hook, join the working yarn to bottom left corner of Strip 1 with a slip stitch. One loop on hook. Holding yarn to back, enter hook from front to back into selvedge on Strip 2. and with yarn still in back enter hook from front to back into selvedge on Strip 1. Grab yarn with hook and pull through Strip1 and Strip 2 to front. Two loops on hook. With yarn in center between both strips, grab yarn and pull through both loops on hook.

Continue to join pieces in this manner, matching pattern squares at their bind off rows. Take into consideration that some squares have different row gauges, correct the alignment by skipping rows on one side or other as needed.

- If yarn tails are at the edges, work them into the seam as you crochet. Or after the seaming is complete use a darning needle to hide them into the crochet edge.

- If yarn tails are one or two sts into the pattern row, do all crochet first then use a darning needle to work them to the seam and hide them into the crochet edge.

After all strips are seamed together work a crochet edge all around in single crochet as below or add any decorative edging of your choice.

Single Crochet Edge (2 rounds)

With RS facing, starting at the bottom right, using crochet hook join yarn (about 1" from corner) to the cast on edge. [*Work 1 sc in next 2 sts, skip next stitch; rep from * to corner. Work 3 sc in corner. Sc into every each selvedge along side edge. Work 3 sc in corner.] Repeat along bind off edge and next side, through corner and join to first sc with a slip stitch. Chain 1. Turn work. Work another round of sc in every sc of previous round, working 3 sc in each corner. Join with a slip stitch and fasten off.

Visit my website www.lisahoffmanknits.com
Follow me on Instagram, Facebook and Ravelry @lisahoffmanknits

The Sampler Blanket by Lisa Hoffman

Row and Repeat Tracker

Make copies of this page to help keep track of rows and pattern repeats.

Patterns 1, 2, 7, 16, 18, 27

	1	2	3	4	5	6	7	8	9	10	11	12
R1												
R2												
R3												
R4												

Pattern 4

	1	2	3	4	5	6	7	8	9	10	11
R1											
R2											
R3											
R4											

Patterns 10, 14

	1	2	3	4	5	6	7	8
R1								
R2								
R3								
R4								
R5								
R6								

Pattern 15

	1	2	3	4	5	6	7	8	9
R1									
R2									
R3									
R4									
R5									
R6									

Pattern 6

	1	2	3	4	5	6	7	8
R1								
R2								
R3								
R4								
R5								
R6								
R7								
R8								

Patterns 3, 12, 13, 20, 21, 22, 28, 29

	1	2	3	4	5	6
R1						
R2						
R3						
R4						
R5						
R6						
R7						
R8						

Pattern 23

	1	2	3	4	5	6	7	8	9	10	11	12
R3												
R4												
R5												
R6												

Patterns 8, 9, 11

	1	2	3	4	5
R1					
R2					
R3					
R4					
R5					
R6					
R7					
R8					
R9					
R10					

Patterns 5, 17, 26, 30

	1	2	3
R1			
R2			
R3			
R4			
R5			
R6			
R7			
R8			
R9			
R10			
R11			
R12			
R13			
R14			
R15			
R16			

Patterns 19, 24, 25

	1	2	3	4
R1				
R2				
R3				
R4				
R5				
R6				
R7				
R8				
R9				
R10				
R11				
R12				

12 Square Sampler Baby Blanket

Use this schematic as a suggestion, or choose patterns of your preference.
Pattern 1 may be worked as Seed Dots or with the same number of sts in
Stockinette St for monogramming.
Finished measurement will be approximately 26" x 32" using a worsted weight yarn.

Purl Triangles Pattern 17	**Harris Tweed** Pattern 24	**Mock Eyelet Cable Rib** Pattern 16
Double Fleck Pattern 27	**Slip Stitch Waffle Rib** Pattern 11	**Mirrored Twists** Pattern 15
Bramble Stitch Pattern 4	**Diamond Brocade** Pattern 20	**Popcorn** Pattern 7
King Charles Brocade Pattern 25	**Knotted Cables** Pattern 5	**Seed Dots** Pattern 1 or **Stockinette Stitch**

NOTES

NOTES

Sampler Baby Blanket knit with Koigu Emmi.

Visit my website www.lisahoffmanknits.com
Follow me on Instagram, Facebook and Ravelry @lisahoffmanknits

The Sampler Blanket by Lisa Hoffman

Copyright 6/2021

Made in the USA
Las Vegas, NV
08 December 2024

13552831R00019